PERFECTLY FLAWED

Uncovering Your

Greatest Purpose

KRISTY LASCHOBER

Perfectly Flawed

© 2023 Kristy Laschober

Photography by Lahna Marie

Cover design by Geo Derice of Firstbookdone.com

ISBN: 979-8-9885184-0-2

Contents

Foreword	7
Perfectly Flawed Intoduction	9
The Beginning	15
Detaching	17
Rebel Rebel	19
Navigating Life	21
Who Am I?	23
Painful Lies	25
Going Backwards	27
Bad Choices	29
Risk	31
Consequences	35
Alone and Lockdown	37
Moments Replayed	39
Fearful and Wonderful Wreck	41
Jesus in Jail	45
Light and Dark	47
Judgment Day	49
Change of Plans	51

Inauthentic	53
Acceptance	55
A Deeper Understanding	57
Another Chance	59
Courage Required	61
Re-Entering	63
Shame Obliterated	65
Destined for Happiness	67
Smarty Pants	69
Letting Go	71
Shawshank Moments	73
Dark and Light are Good	75
Using My Voice	77
Mentorship	79
The Freedom Exchange Project Conversations	81
I'm a Complex Human - The Journey Continues	83
Some Final Thoughts	85
Journaling Section	87

They say that when a person is incarcerated, their family does the time with them.
It's sad but true.
That's why this page is extra special to write.
I get to, in public, express my sincere gratitude for the vast love that never faltered.

♥

Thank you to my beautiful mother Sharon,
for being the ultimate, fierce advocate from day one.

Thank you to my extraordinary sister Tamara, my ultimate ride-or-die,
who taught me higher consciousness living.

Thank you to Dave, the best brother-in-law I could have ever asked for.

Thank you to McKane and Hayden, my favorite young men.

Thank you to my Father in Heaven, for showering me with agape love,
on earth and beyond.

Thank you to Federal Judge Ann Aiken
who believed in me from the first day of reentry court.

And lastly,

Thank you to all my beautiful friends and mentors along the way,
who revealed their perceived flaws, and loved every part of me every day,
when I wasn't sure how I felt about myself.

XO Kristy

Foreword

I will always remember that Fall Sunday morning when a dear friend approached me, walking next to a woman I had never seen before.

"Gina this is Kristy and Kristy this is Gina," he said. "I think you two should know each other."

I think about that moment from time to time, and it still makes me smile. I wasn't aware that Kristy had called my friend from prison, knowing he had moved to Ashland, Oregon, where she would be relocating when she got out. She asked him if he knew of a woman who could mentor her. And just like that, Kristy and I found ourselves at the beginning of a beautiful journey.

We connected in a 12-step program. I watched as my new friend bravely shared her fear out loud, in front of the whole room, and recounted the experiences that led her there. You could hear a pin drop. Kristy commanded the room when she spoke - not because she was pushy but because she was authentic and full of hope. Even today, that beautiful hope and authenticity are stirring up new friendships and opening new doors. Kristy is a force in the world and it has been my honor to mentor her.

It wasn't an easy road for Kristy. I recall her looking around her new community of Ashland with a lack of enthusiasm and saying, "Why do I have to live here?"

"You GET to live here," I would remind her.

Ashland and the wonderful people living there were the perfect recipes for healing and growth. Kristy dug into the hard work and became deeply connected to her authentic self, right before my eyes. It was pure joy to behold. When she was called to move to New Orleans, I knew I would miss her, but what a thrill it was to cheer her on as she continued her adventure.

Some may think of this as a story about Kristy. Well, it is not. This is a story about us - all of us who have been hurt and have flaws in all their glory. Each imperfection, each perceived defect, and weakness has the potential to make us stronger. We all have the opportunity to get to know ourselves to our deepest core. And most importantly, regardless of the season we find ourselves in, we all have the power and choice to remain teachable.

If you are reading this, then you have one of the best gifts you could give yourself. Read this with an open mind and you will be surprised where you will go. Kristy has shared an intimate part of herself so that we can all grow into who we are supposed to be.

I do want you to remember something as you open these pages and do the work. Taking an honest look into every part of your life is an emotionally tense process. Kristy is sharing her personal experience with you because she now knows that sharing, exposing, and excavating various nuances of her life - bringing the darkness out into the light - is what gave her true freedom. It is an intense process, but so worth it! And there are things you can put into place right now that will help the process.

- Given the depth of emotional responses required, Kristy and I recommend not rushing through your process. Write a little and stop if you want to.
- Allow yourself to cry as much as you feel like it. Releasing your emotions is healthy.
- Be really kind to yourself. Getting to our authentic selves can be exhausting.
- Perhaps work through one chapter a week and take time to reflect and process with a trusted friend. Having a person to share your process with is vital.
- Choose someone who has already started the journey of self-reflection so that they don't project their unhealed pain on you.

I have so much joy in mentoring Kristy and other women like us because it keeps me mindful of my blessings. I get to practice my appreciation for life and forgiveness for others, including myself. Today I live with a peaceful mind and joy in my heart, and I wish that for you as well. I commend you on your choice to pick up this book and do the hard work. May you find the freedom, hope, and connection you're looking for.

Gina DuQuenne

Perfectly Flawed

Uncovering Your Greatest Purpose

Introduction

The first time I heard the three words, "flawed human being," I was sitting in a circle of 23 women in a cramped room with bright fluorescent lights, right in the center of a maximum security federal prison in Texas. I was told I was a "flawed human being" and I was immediately defensive. After all, I had worked hard all my life at not revealing my flaws. Flaws were a sign of weakness, a shameful burden to bear. Yet here I was, in a notorious prison drug program, being forced to face the fact that I was flawed. It wrecked me.

That's when I started to write in a journal. I had to learn about myself. We have all heard that writing is good for us. That writing will bring out healing and creativity. That it will set us free.

Most of us already have journals and some of them have a few words written down too. Our intentions are good. We want to heal. But where do we start?

Why is it so dang hard?

Writing can be daunting and scary for most of us, but have you ever asked yourself why? After all, it's just a piece of paper and an ink pen.

I can tell you why it was hard for me. **I was afraid.** I didn't admit it at the time, but looking back I know that I was afraid.

Afraid to get too close to the woman I was supposed to be.

Afraid to take responsibility for my choices and mistakes.

Afraid to tap into the parts of myself I didn't like. The parts that I judged. The parts of me that I didn't want anyone to see.

Did you know that when we judge a person or behavior, we are actually revealing the way we see ourselves? Our own judgmental attitude is rarely about someone else.

It's almost always about us.

What if we could love people for who they are - as they are - and seek to better understand ourselves? What if we could unlock the secrets about why we do the things we don't want to do? What if we could accept, and even learn to embrace, our humanity in all of its beauty and flaws? After all, I am a flawed human being. And so are you.

To be clear, I never thought I was perfect. Far from it. I wouldn't even call myself a perfectionist. So why was it so difficult for me to admit I was flawed?

I knew I was a good person. I was generous and loving and smart. But I also committed a crime and was sentenced to 5 years in federal prison. Could I be both good and flawed at the same time? My mind couldn't accept it. There was a disconnect somewhere and I had to figure it out.

I purchased a black and white notebook from commissary and began to ask myself questions. Lots of questions. Deep questions. And I forced myself to respond with honest answers. That was the difficult part. I eventually learned an important lesson.

Every answer I seek lies within myself.

The perfect answer to every question we have is inside of us, oftentimes trapped by old conditioning and survival techniques we've learned from a young age.

Here's what else I've come to know - it doesn't matter how good or challenging our upbringing was, we all still have stuff to unravel in order to get to our true authentic self.

Why is it so important to get back to her?

Because she was born for greatness. We were never meant to be weighed down by all that we have been forced to carry. We were meant for love and freedom and a ton of grace. Grace for ourselves and grace for others.

Freedom lies within us, and it launches us toward exactly who we were meant to be.

Starting right there in prison I began my journey back to myself. Embracing the challenging parts of my character was the first step. Loving all of Kristy. Every single solitary part of who I am was the key. Not hiding it. Bringing it all out to the light was the greatest gift writing gave me. Because I had already cultivated a spiritual relationship with God, I wasn't alone in this quest.

I gave my journaled answers lots of GRACE and was determined to be truthful. For someone like me who didn't like journaling, I am fascinated by the fact that I still, six years later, write almost every morning. It's a date I have with myself because I'm my most important relationship. I am my best friend and the only way to have a healthy relationship is honest communication.

Isn't that true freedom?

The freedom I've obtained from writing is incredible.

I want every person I come in contact with to be free.

My joy is to pass on the gift I received.

This book you hold in your hand is actually a personal invitation. It doesn't tell my entire story, but bite-sized pieces of truth that I've learned, some of them in different locations during my journey. I'm hoping you find a little of your own journey somehow in these pages.

I invite you to be brave and to trust me. Let's be transparent together. Let's walk together on this beautiful writing journey.

Take my hand .. let's go, beautiful friend. You are not alone.

This is a good spot to tape a picture of yourself at a younger age.

We are on our way back to the little beautiful human that loved to play and discover and act silly.

If you don't have a picture you can draw right here. Draw something you used to love doing.

The Beginning

I was born into this world as a beautiful being with endless possibilities. Just like you. We relied on our parents or caretakers to nurture us and allow us to bloom into the unique personality we are all blessed with. I remember being happy, I think. I was told I was a happy baby and that my father would come home from his bartending job late at night and wake me up just so he could play with me.

When I was born, my body wasn't like others. I was born with birth defects. That's what they used to call them in 1965. I'd like to use different words but then it feels as if I'm trying to make it pretty. The words sound so ugly and flawed and wrong. Maybe it was way back then that my little spirit decided to fight. Maybe that's where my denial began to kick in - pretending that I was normal. That I didn't have a small thumb on one hand and no thumb on the other. Pretending that my insides were the same as everyone else. Pretending that it didn't bother me. That's a big revelation as I write this.

My mother talks about my grandparents being too afraid to babysit me. Even in my young mind, something didn't add up. Birth defect? My heart felt normal, my silliness and adventuresome spirit didn't feel defective. Maybe that's where I started to believe that something was wrong with me.

How did you enter this world?

When did you begin believing certain things about yourself?

How does this affect your life? (write your reflections on pages 88-89)

DETACHING

I spent much of my childhood in and out of the hospital. I think that's where I learned to get along with other kids and where I mastered my people-pleasing skills. Every time I was admitted into CHOC (Children's Hospital of Orange County), I was placed in a room with three to five other children.

I was an observer, acutely aware of my surroundings. I watched how others interacted with the nurses and doctors and I could never understand why they acted out the way they did. Why did they have to cry and scream? Why did they bite the nurses? I was appalled at their willingness to express and act out their true emotions. I didn't have that ability, nor did I want it.

I was proud of the way I behaved - nice, calm, and polite. I was different, and my positive demeanor provided rewards that only reinforced the appropriate display of certain emotions.

Nurses used to rub my back with lotion at night and brought dolls in for me to play with. I understood, even at such a young age, that I needed them to protect me and to give me my pain shots in a timely manner. *Every four hours.* I received massive amounts of drugs into my little body every four hours and that's what kept me okay with what was happening. I could get numb this way and use it as an extraordinary coping mechanism.

I believe this is where I detached from myself. I didn't know that's what I was doing and it took me going to prison before I realized that I left myself in order to survive. I'm learning that I am not alone in this act.

When a child experiences trauma, escaping is automatic. It wasn't my fault. Escaping and detaching is a normal reaction that isn't talked about in great length. As I got older I thought that something was wrong with me because I internalized my ability to not give a shit as avoidance or denial. Like it was a bad thing.

This swirl of a perfect storm is how the trajectory of addiction and rebellion started for me.

On days I was released from the hospital I was given a huge bottle of pain pills and instructions to take it easy for a while.

"Be careful of the stitches," they would warn.

I mostly didn't listen.

I never let authoritative rules hold me back.

If I wanted to go to the beach I did. If I wanted to ride my bike fast or eat spicy foods,

I did. This pattern would eventually lead me to places I never wanted to go.

What pain or trauma did you experience as a child?

What tools did you use to survive?

Do you still use those tools and do they still serve you?

What new insight do you have thinking back on those days? Is this connecting any dots for you?

Write about it all with lots of GRACE and no judgment. (write your reflections on pages 90-91)

Rebel Rebel

I've always had good friends. That's why I thought it would be easy to find more when I moved in the 8th grade. The principal assigned a student to befriend me because it was a new community. It's funny how I still remember her name. Sabrina ditched me right away. I sat by myself at lunch for the next few months until I met a couple of girls who I'm still friends with today.

Shortly after, I began dabbling with weed. It was out of curiosity and I liked that I could change the way I felt like I could with pain pills. In high school, my interest in mind-altering substances continued.

There was one time in particular that I got in trouble for coming home drunk, after I was supposed to be at a high school event. My next-door neighbor bought us alcohol and I distinctly remember asking him how many beers it would take for me to get drunk. I was wearing brand new, stark white jeans when I slid down a hill of mud as we hid from the police who were called to the school. I also started my period, so you can imagine what a mess I was.

I had never seen my father so angry in my life. He called me names I'd rather not repeat and then apologized the next day on our way to church.

Needless to say I was grounded for a long time after that. Being on restriction simply put a pause on the trajectory of where I was headed. There was a liquor store near the mall a couple of miles away where we could get alcohol on a whim, anytime. A secret door in the back of the building is how we entered once Ken (the owner) saw who we were. There were about 50 of us who were permitted all access all the time.

A long, running tab was not uncommon and in the evening each of us would write down all the parties we knew about on a large chalkboard. There were sofas and tables where we could hang out if we wanted.

At the time I thought we were the cool kids. But now, looking back, I see how Ken took advantage of us and how he criminally contributed to the delinquency of minors. Most of us were between the ages of 16-18 years old. We could drink alcohol during school, on the way to the beach, and definitely at night before and after parties. Although I had strict parents, it was easy to swing by Kens before we went anywhere.

I don't know why I was so enamored by the special treatment we received. I loved having other options than pain medication to deal with unwanted emotions and the freedom to express the wild side of me.

I think I also loved the excitement of getting away with stuff. I was never a rule follower. I enjoyed the act of pushing limits and teetering on the edge.

My parents had strict rules about getting good grades because they knew I was smart. I did minimal effort, probably because I didn't like to be forced.

My high school teachers were overly friendly and generously gave my girlfriends and I their cars to drive to the beach whenever we wanted. They wrote us notes to get out of class, provided us with drugs at their house, took us to concerts and accompanied us on vacations.

I thought it was fun and exciting but again, as I reflect back as an adult, I see that they were simply disgusting predators. Slowly, the pattern of my life was weaving itself into something that would cost me everything to shake off.

What do you remember most about your teenage years?

Were you rebellious?

Did you follow the rules? Why?

What was your motivation for the way you lived your life?

Did adults take advantage of you, with or without you realizing it? (write your reflections on pages 92-93)

Navigating Life

After I graduated high school, I traveled for the first time to Europe. I'd been out of the country to Mexico and loved the adventure of traveling. I worked two jobs at once to save as much as I could and then went on a backpacking trip throughout Europe. When I had a particular goal I was excited about, I was tenacious beyond measure. It was fun saving money and working as many hours as I could.

In between travels I attended college for fashion merchandising and sprinkled in hospital visits for weeks at a time to address my physical condition. At the same time, I experimented with mind-altering substances and stayed out much too late, and it affected my school work. I used my medical issues as an excuse to let my schoolwork fall behind and miss important tests.

Even though I struggled with health issues, I wasn't consistent in school. I wish I was more conscientious, but I was still looking at authority and rules as outside of myself and something to manipulate, not having a clue that I was only hurting me.

I met and got married to a man that I thought would tame my wild side. We dated for four years and my father and he got along famously. He didn't have a father he could look up to and my dad didn't have a son he could go fishing with so they became fast friends. Shortly after our wedding, he became an Orange County Sheriff, and we were excited about his new career.

My parents had divorced and my father remarried a woman that was hard for me to love. I didn't like that the attention he used to have for me was centered on her. She had three younger kids and they were all living together. The tension between my parents and my father's new wife was volatile to say the least, particularly when I was admitted into the hospital.

It was brutal.

My mom was sad and my dad wasn't showing up as much and I felt torn because of the guilt about being sick again. My medical situation caused tension, pain, and literal anguish. I hated the feeling of being caged in and at the mercy of my family's heightened emotions. The only way I knew how to deal with it was through disconnecting from myself and numbing through potent morphine and demerol.

I didn't know how to set boundaries and because I knew that they loved me and were sacrificing for me, I internalized it all and I kept using pills after I was released from the hospital.

Pills and emotions were synonymous for me, and I was determined to manage them myself.

Don't like this emotion? Take a pill (or 4 pills).

Need to set a boundary but don't know how? Take 5 pills.

What started as a temporary way to get through my day began to take over my life, one pill at a time.

How did you navigate life with uncomfortable emotions?

What were the ups and downs of your experience?

What were your examples of marriage?

How did you approach your partnerships? (write your reflections on pages 94-95)

Who Am I?

My husband was a rule follower and liked things a certain way. Do you have anyone in your life who is that way? Or maybe that describes you.

Since I was used to acquiescing to others, it wasn't hard for me to comply with anything my husband wanted from me. I put my needs aside most of the time and obviously it didn't make for a deep and intimate relationship.

On days I had doctor visits, he would ask if I wanted him to come and I said I'd rather go by myself. I found it stressful to manage his feelings. It wasn't that he had asked me to, but I had experienced many moments of getting into the elevator to see a doctor and feeling the anxiety of whomever I was with while they talked themselves through every medical outcome of my experience. I would stand quietly and stare forward while they prepared themselves for the worst. I didn't know how to say I didn't like that, and so I learned it was just easier to go to doctor appointments alone.

I was always told that I could have children, but at 27 I had too many cysts and complications and the only way to stop it was to have a hysterectomy and take everything out.

Because the sadness was so great, I detached from my reality even further and quickly agreed to the operation. The next day one of the attending physicians came to see me.

"I wanted to meet you," she said. "You have had so many operations in your young life that I just wanted to meet you."

"Not really," I said quickly. "I haven't been through that much."

When the words came out of my mouth I felt stupid. Why would I say that? I had been through a lot. I should have just smiled and said thank you. That would have been a normal and healthy way to reply. Like a knee-jerk reaction, I responded in a way that would make her more comfortable and make me seem normal - *unflawed*.

She had the most quizzical look on her face as she smiled and patted my arm.

"Well I think you're an extraordinary young lady and I just wanted to meet you," she said.

That whole afternoon I thought about my reaction and wondered why I felt the need to respond that way. I was embarrassed. Looking back, I can see it furthered my belief that something must be wrong with me.

Four years after our wedding, I went to rehab. My addiction was profound and I had gotten pulled over by my husband's sergeant while intoxicated.

Rehab worked. It was a whole new world, being sober.

In the beginning, I took Vitamin C as a replacement for the act of taking pills. My emotions were heightened and I submerged myself into a 12-step program. I relapsed one time, a month after my first attempt at sobriety because I couldn't imagine going on a houseboat in the middle of a lake with my family and no pills. I was terrified.

I went to work at a law firm while I started a wardrobe styling business and I loved them both.

After a few years of maintaining my sobriety my husband and I decided to adopt. We learned about the process, created a profile, did a home study, and trudged through all of the paperwork.

There was a lot of unspoken pain, and underneath my smiles and excitement, I began to crack.

How do other people see you?

Does it line up with who you actually are?

What parts of you do you hide? (write your reflections on pages 96-97)

Painful Lies

It was New Year's Eve and my eyebrows needed waxed. We were going to celebrate at home with spaghetti carbonara and a buttery loaf of garlic bread. My husband was picking up a movie, so I had a little time.

Laying on the table of the Brow Bar that was just a mile up from the beach, I heard my phone ring. Damn, I forgot to turn off the ringer. The ringing was incessant. The aesthetician paused and looked at me with a look on her face that said, "You gonna pick that up?" I apologized and grabbed my phone just as the same number called my phone again.

"Hello, yes, hi, is this Kristy?"

"Yes, it is."

"Well, my name is Kristy too. And I am in love with your husband."

Huh?

"We are in love. We've been seeing each other for months and I just thought you should know."

She was drunk, that much was clear to me.

I slowly put down the phone dumbfounded at what I just heard. My husband would never do that, I thought. Immediately, moments started flooding my brain. Times when he was too tired to go do anything fun, or when we were on our way to our adoption interview and he was talking like he wasn't sure anymore.

Then that time on the cruise ship when he holed up in the room reading because his job as a police officer was taking a toll on him.

I always made excuses for him because I couldn't admit that he wasn't into me like that anymore. He used the word TIRED like a badge of honor to refrain from participating in any meaningful activity. This slowly became the norm after I got sober.

Damn. Is this really happening? Now I had to face and confront an impossible situation. I hate confrontation. I never learned how to do it appropriately. Now would have been a great time to pop a few pills to give me courage and step into the bold person I could be when I was altered.

I laid back down on the table so she could finish the other eyebrow.

It's funny, right? Making sure my eyebrows are on point. For what? To face a cheating husband?

I am surprised by how easily I can detach from my body, allowing me to turn off bad feelings like a water faucet. It was almost like I didn't just hear that my world was going to change forever, except for that fiery burn running through my body, cutting off air to my throat.

It's an off-switch I have instant access to when I don't want to think about something facing me that's too big and that I know will cause me pain.

Anger is a color in my crayon box I threw away a long time ago. Anger wasn't safe or accepted or appropriate. I'm sure that's why I didn't get angry.

I met him at the house, told him about the call and really I don't remember exactly what was said, except that he said he didn't love her.

Then his phone rang and I knew it was the other Kristy (she probably spells it Cristi or something stupid).

He looked at me and I said, "You're not going to answer that right?"

He did.

I left.

Not long after that, my father passed away from cancer.

My husband and I separated and I decided to fost-adopt a child on my own.

Emotions were taking over my mind and body and I used my off switch so as not to deal with any of it. It barely worked. And then it stopped working.

Grief was a more powerful force. I needed something stronger to help me reign in my emotions.

I was cracking.

What do you do when you are faced with something painful?

How easily do you have access to your emotions?

What are those emotions?

What emotions have you thrown away a long time ago? (write your reflections on pages 98-99)

Going Backwards

After we separated I started dating a man named Chad who I had been friends with. He also suffered from addiction but was sober when we met. We had fun together. He was wild and free and loved to travel. It was not uncommon for him to send me a text message photo of a villa in Tuscany with the words *let's go*.

It was also not uncommon for him to relapse every few months. It was hard because in a way I understood. Again, I made excuses for him. This was the first time I'd been on the other side of loving someone who was addicted. It was very painful.

On a bright sunny day during one of those relapses, I was admitted into Hoag hospital in Newport Beach, CA, where my room had a view of the sparkling blue ocean. My kidneys were acting up and I was laying in bed, alone, thinking.

I was thinking about my father being in the same hospital getting chemo a few years back. Thinking about how much I missed him because he died anyway. And thinking about how much I hated hospitals.

I was mad that I was sitting there alone. Where was Chad?

A beautiful and terrible thought landed in my head like a tornado. A dilaudid shot would help me get through this. I used to carry those pills around with me everywhere, before I got sober. They were a part of my past, but also ingrained in who I was.

The thought marinated in my head for a while, and then the nurse popped in to check my IV.

"Would you like a pain shot Kristen?"

There it was. Like the devil handing me relief on a shiny, silver platter.

I took the deepest breath of my life and said, "Yes."

Dilaudid, shooting straight into my veins always had a way of making everything in my world okay. Immediately after the nurse left to go get a syringe, my entire body began to relax. I took the deepest breath I could possibly take, anticipating the feeling of euphoria I'd soon be experiencing.

While waiting for the nurse to arrive with a syringe filled with peace, I thought about my sobriety. Up to this point, I had several years of continuous sobriety. I was extremely proud of that fact. I had a wonderful sponsor and sponsored several girls. My sponsor was at the hospital visiting me the night before.

Do I really need a pain shot? The answer was uncomfortable. It was simply, NO.

But at that moment I didn't care. I wanted relief. I deserved some relief, dammit!

My father was dead. I recently and successfully went through open heart surgery. I was now in the hospital again for my kidneys and my boyfriend was probably using drugs in Palm Springs.

Life was getting hard again. I should be stronger. I should reach out to my sponsor. I should.

I pushed those thoughts of sobriety away when I heard my nurse coming down the hall and my heart began to flutter.

"In less than 60 Seconds I will be happy," I told myself.

I could stop worrying about everything and just enjoy the feeling.

"Sorry it took me so long Kristen," the nurse said.

"That's okay," I said meekly. It was strange - I was already feeling high before the needle even went in.

I kept my eyes closed and began to feel the warmth in my veins. Oh, how I loved that feeling. My whole body began to relax. This was going to be a good dose, I thought. Then my head swirled a little and I felt it in my throat.

She pulled back the syringe and quietly said, "Okay Kristen you should start feeling better. Let me know if you need anything."

I just smiled and said, "Okay thank you," while a salty tear ran down my face.

Can you recall a time when you said okay to something you knew you shouldn't have?

What was your motivation?

Were the consequences high?

How long did it take to recover from that decision?

How have you experienced addiction? (write your reflections on pages 100-101)

Bad Choices

I never meant to become a drug dealer. I loved being a wardrobe stylist, but because I started using drugs I was inconsistent with my regular clients, even though I adored them. Let me back up a second.

My boyfriend Chad relapsed and I went to Palm Springs to help him. I also made an excruciatingly stupid decision. I was honestly worried about my recent relapse I'd set into motion with my pill addiction, so I decided to try meth. That was Chad's drug of choice. It seems unthinkable, but at the time it made sense to me. You see, when I was released from the hospital, they sent me on my way with 100 vicodin and I knew I wouldn't be able to stop. I liked the way meth made me feel and I honestly didn't think I'd get addicted. Throw some ghb in the mix, something new I decided to try, and I was hooked.

When my boyfriend found out I tried methamphetamine he was furious. I can't emphasize that enough. I had never seen him so upset. He was practically snot crying and yelling at the same time, "Kristy you are supposed to be the light! This is the devil! I don't want you a part of this. OH MY GOD what did you do?"

He held his face in his hands, rocking back and forth while we sat on the back patio. I didn't quite understand. I really thought he was just being dramatic. He didn't understand that I was trying to stop my addiction from taking me down. As I said, it made sense to me.

After a long while, he settled into the fact that I was in his world now. We bought extra so we could sell some and pay less.

As you can imagine, I have so many stories woven into the tapestry of being a drug dealer. I did not belong in that world. Neither of us did, but we were. I transferred my skills as a wardrobe stylist entrepreneur into buying and selling narcotics. We were deeply involved with people from Mexico and I found myself navigating a foreign business.

Once, I reprimanded our supplier for being late and he reminded me that with the massive amounts of money and drugs he was bringing me to the rented Palm Springs house, he would not be on a schedule that could be followed by anyone. He brought to my attention the fact that people get killed in these scenarios all the time. His statement hit me in the gut ... hard. I was not buying and selling shoes at Nordstrom like I used to. I was buying drugs from another country. Holy shit. I was selling drugs.

We had people we sold to in our area and spent a lot of time in Palm Springs, but our big client was a catholic priest from Connecticut. He would come to be known as Monsignor Meth.

Did the magnitude of bad choices ever hit you?

How did you block it out?

Did someone close to you ever make bad choices?

How did you deal with it? (write your reflections on pages 102-103)

Risk

A year after my release from prison (you'll read more about that later) I received a call from a friend of a friend about writing a Vagina Monologue. The theme was women and prison and they asked if I would participate. Because I made a commitment to myself to say yes as often as possible, I said YES. I didn't think I knew how to write a monologue but I drafted some words and a month later it was performed on stage. The monologue ends with my prison experience beginning. I thought this would be a good place to let you read it, so here it is.

My vagina has been locked away since the morning I was arrested.

Right up until the very second federal agents forced their way into my hotel room my vagina was happy, peaceful, warm, safe, and extremely satisfied.

Sex with your partner on the eve of being thrown to the floor and shackled is not a common experience.

Exposed and having no idea what was happening, my vagina remained in a blissful and ignorant state ... for the next few hours.

A pink leopard nightie was the only veil protecting my vagina from the invasion of coarse carpet fibers, trying to get close. Butted up against it.

My vagina was no longer free. It was the property of the United States Government. All of me was.

My vagina had never been in trouble before or seen the inside of a jail.

Well, that's not entirely true.

When I was married to a police officer my vagina would go inside the jails to bring him a homemade lunch. I was a good wife.

But he had an affair.

And I got caught selling drugs to a priest with my boyfriend.

My vagina and I were in big trouble.

I tried to stop using drugs but I just couldn't.

Not even the success and love of my fabulous wardrobe styling business could stop me from damaging my vagina.

I dressed the best vaginas in silk and French lace and the softest denim you could imagine.

After I relapsed and began doing meth my vagina came alive. It took on a life of its own, a force to be reckoned with.

My vagina begged for attention and became a willing slave to euphoria.

But after so long, my vagina got scared, nervous.

This was just supposed to be for fun. Not a lifestyle.

But I couldn't stop using drugs.

The marshals let me cover my vagina with a pair of leggings. I was shaking too violently to put on underwear.

My vagina was innocent. My vagina did not deserve to be treated like a criminal.

You would think after four years in prison they would stop accusing my vagina but they didn't.

My vagina has never been a temporary home to drugs or any other paraphernalia.

Lift your breasts.	Oh no here it comes.
Turn around.	I didn't do it.
Bend at the waist.	Please don't look.
Spread your butt cheeks.	I'm innocent.
Give two hard coughs.	Maybe they'll stop here.
Spread your vagina lips.	Idiots
Give two hard coughs.	Assholes.

Writing a monologue was a creative way to describe a traumatic experience from a sacred body part. I'm so glad I said yes to something I thought I had no business doing. I'm learning that the more open I am to new opportunities, the more I can heal from unlikely sources. God has a way of helping me heal through ways I would have never imagined. Saying YES to what He has for me and being observant at what comes out of it, allows me to take life a little less seriously and trust an entity more powerful than myself.

Are you open to new opportunities presented to you?

Write about a time you took a risk and said YES.

What impact did it have? (write your reflections on pages 104-105)

Consequences

I was not prepared for my consequences of committing a crime. My brain short circuited and I left reality. I started hallucinating, seeing things that weren't there and knowing I was slipping into altered states but not having a clue how to get out of it. I have glimpses of a memory of being dressed in a paper gown, housed in a small cell that had a tiny window in the door. An officer was peering in, anytime I opened my eyes. He was yelling words at me but I don't know what they were. I was told they sent me to the hospital for a week but I do not remember any of that either. When I got back to Pahrump Detention Center in Nevada, I settled in my new space for a few weeks. The unit was a big dorm-style room with beds in a linear fashion. The other women inside had told me I'd be leaving on Con-air soon but I didn't believe them. How could there really be a plane called Con-air? But they were right. I was to put back on my clothes I was arrested in - brown, fitted leggings and a short-sleeved camouflage print t-shirt - preparing to be black-boxed shackled like an evil woman who couldn't be trusted.

The men in custody were already on the plane before the women could board. We were instructed to keep our eyes forward and not talk to or acknowledge any of the males. The plane was full and I didn't know if Chad would be on that flight. The last time I saw him was when we laid face down on the carpet in the Las Vegas hotel room as the marshalls put the handcuffs on. The front two rows were empty and I sat where they told me. Tears started streaming down my eyes when I saw that I was to sit directly in front of Chad. The feeling of seeing him shackled was indescribable. The Marshal sat in the front row turning to face me. His eyes were on all of us, there wasn't a way I could say anything to Chad or him to me. After an hour of settling in and not knowing exactly where they were taking us, I leaned to the right as if I was trying to find a comfortable place to rest my head on the seat. The black box I was attached to automatically moved with me, with the heavy chain around my waist, and I was able to touch the knee of Chad's jeans between me and the seat next to me. I kept my finger there the entire plane ride, scratching the small tear, listening to us both weeping. This was real and there was no way to get out of it or go back or make a different decision.

As we began our descent I asked the Marshal where we were landing and he said he couldn't tell me. We had been up in the air for probably three or four hours and I assumed we were somewhere close to Connecticut. We landed on the outskirts of an airport with armed guards waiting for us. *Was this all really necessary,* I thought? It was snowing heavily when they ordered the men to evacuate the plane first. This would be the last time I would see Chad for a long time.

We were standing shackled in the middle of a blizzard and I was freezing. The Marshals had full snow gear on including face masks that only revealed their eyes. The few women were ordered to line up on one side of the plane, opposite the men. Chad asked if he could give me his sweatshirt but they said no. Was this legal? I guess it didn't really matter. I was the property of the Federal Government.

The men got into separate vans based on where the Marshals sent them. We still didn't know where we were. After a while, I was the only one left standing in the blizzard. I later found out that the facility that was supposed to get me had forgotten so they ultimately took me with the rest of the women to Danbury Federal Prison.

Write about a time you were facing the unknown or faced circumstances that were out of your control.

How did you feel?

What did you do? (write your reflections on pages 106-107)

Alone and Lockdown

*I**Pod*. I called it iPod. That was the name of the unit I was assigned to at Donald Wyatt Detention Center in Rhode Island. I have to admit learning that I was on my way up to iPod gave me a silly, sad smile at the irony of never seeing my own iPods again, and instead LIVING in an iPod. This was a big moment, preparing to enter the room I would call home for the next couple of years. Some of these women I was about to meet, I'd be friends with for many years after. I would cry and laugh and experience deep pain with these ladies but, of course, I didn't know that at the time.

My legs would not stop shaking as I stepped out of the elevator onto the freshly waxed floors and looked around at the muddy beige concrete hallway. Every door was a heavily locked, armored entrance that had to be buzzed open by another officer. Every door.

A shrieking sound came as the first door opened. I was told to wait while the women in the day room were told to "rack-up." This entrance was not a way for me to make friends. I heard moaning and irritation while cards were thrown on the table because their game was interrupted. Some of the women were watching Ellen and they were vocally angry they couldn't finish the show. *They already hated me*, I thought. I took a deep breath.

My duffle bag was emptied into a cell and I was told to enter. An older, short CO (Corrections Officer) was at the desk and she was asking me questions when the door opened and another inmate with long, scraggly gray hair walked through. They didn't seem to mind her being there. With me sitting in the cell, shaking, hoping I'd only have to be there for a few hours, the woman walked by me slowly and began saying something. I shook my head, trying to focus on her words.

"They are going to lock you down for three days, but they aren't going to tell you that," she said flatly. "Don't worry, you'll be okay. They won't give you a pencil or paper, but I will try to sneak one in for you. The food will be disgusting without any seasoning but you'll get some when you get out. Try to sleep and don't let your mind go crazy. I'll try to roll something for you under the door."

And then she walked away. My first thought wasn't fear, it was confusion. This lady obviously didn't know that I wasn't a hardened criminal. I wasn't going to be in this place very long. I'm a polite wardrobe stylist who got caught up in something. I shrugged and smiled at her ignorance as the CO proceeded to approach the door. She gave me a wide smile and then reached over and slammed the door. The skinny, scary woman was right. I was in lockdown.

For the next three days, I was alone in a 6x8 foot cell with a stainless steel sink and toilet. I couldn't sleep and the food was terrible. Occasionally a pencil or piece of paper or a salt packet would slide under my door and I knew it was the kindness of the skinny woman. Once in a while I would look up and see an angry and curious face peering at me in the small window of my cell. Loneliness hovered in an extraordinary way. No birds chirping, no phones ringing, only thoughts of shame and fear.

On the third day, my door buzzed open. I sat paralyzed. I willed myself to stand up and I took a deep breath, ignoring my wobbly legs. *I've got this,* I thought. About 20 women were sitting throughout the unit at different tables. I sat at an empty table not knowing if I should smile or act tough. I stared at the TV instead.

Over the next few months, I became acquainted with most of the women. This was a pre-trial facility so there was a lot of speculation about everyone's future. Heaviness hung in the air while we tried to make it a home. We did a pretty good job, considering all the pain in the room.

Write about a time someone unexpectedly showed you kindness.

Have you ever had to make an unusual place a home? (write your reflections on pages 108-109)

Moments Replayed

The sun was shining, so I knew it had to be daylight. I wondered how long I had been laying on the floor? I had on a purple tank top and panties. The glass kitchen table was inches from my head, and I rolled over and sat up slowly, looking over my body for bruises or blood. Nothing. I slowly got up, turned to the right, and stared into the large mirror in my dining room. I didn't recognize myself. My hair was long with wild curls. I peered into my hollow eyes as tears rolled down my cheeks. How did I get here?

A lot of thoughts go through your head when you are alone with yourself in a prison cell, and this memory was one of them. For a while, when I first woke up every morning, it took me a minute to realize where I was. My chest would immediately feel heavy and a rush of emotion and shame would flood my heart. Deciphering past decisions was not an easy task. I'm not an evil person, yet I was selling drugs to people who were addicted. I was a person with abundant opportunity, but I had chosen to commit a crime. I had loving parents and a beautifully kind sister, so why didn't I stop or ask for help? I knew damn well I wasn't living in integrity, but I just couldn't stop. Why?

Stopping would have required me to face certain truths that I wasn't prepared to face. There were so many times I had a specific moment where my gut was screaming.

STOP. Kristy, you don't belong here. What the hell are you doing?

I thought of the other moments as shame washed over me again and again. Getting held up at gunpoint on three different occasions. Eating Denny's food on Christmas morning with Chad. That morning at Denny's in San Clemente, CA may not seem like a big deal, but it was. Christmas was special in my family and I had missed my flight the day before and rather than joyously running down the stairs to watch my nephews open presents and participate in making a delicious family style breakfast, I was alone, with Chad ordering sub-par food from Denny's. Shame and guilt permeated my body so I kept using drugs. I couldn't get out. My parents worked so hard at keeping me alive and I was actively killing myself.

I replayed those moments and more, as I sat in my prison cell. All of my dirty, dark secrets bubbled up to the surface and they were just hanging out for the world to see.

Write about a particularly poignant moment, when you knew you should stop a behavior.

Does this quote ring true?

"I know I'm doing something wrong and I feel guilty but neither of those things matters enough for me to stop" (write your reflections on pages 110-111)

Fearful and Wonderful Wreck

April 12th was the day I went to court to plead guilty. It was also the day I would be released to the Salvation Army for three months. Walking into the courtroom shackled was an odd and surreal experience. Who was I? I must not be a good person.

After I plead guilty I was escorted back to the holding cell while I waited for what seemed like forever. There are never any clocks to look at when you are in a holding cell and watches aren't allowed. A tall good-looking man walked through the doors with a handful of keys, he told me to turn around and lift my ankles one at a time, so that he could unlock the shackles. Next, I held out my arms so the handcuffs could be removed. I rubbed my wrists attempting to smooth out the dented marks the metal made. Was it necessary to squeeze them that tight?

Instead of closing the door, this time he backed up and raised his left arm as if motioning me to exit the holding cell. It had been four months, almost to the day, since I was allowed to walk free somewhere. My attorney Frank met me in the lobby and I followed him out the door through a long hallway.

He said "I bet you're hungry, what do you want to eat? You want to go to Subway?"

Personally, I'm not a fan of Subway but I wasn't about to be picky.

"Yes, Subway sounds great," I said.

There is no way to describe that feeling of having choices once again. There I stood in a fast food restaurant in Connecticut, dressed in a prison uniform, staring at a bar filled with lettuce, olives, cheese, pickles, and tomatoes. I wanted everything. He told me to order a large and pick out some chips and a soda. We sat down and ate as he was trying to make light conversation. But before we were done he warned me that an opportunity at the Salvation Army was serious. How I spent my time there will determine my success in the future.

I listened but I wasn't really hearing him. I was still trying to get comfortable with sunshine, large windows, and being free again. Being *sober* and free again. It had been many years. I wondered if Frank knew what a wreck I was on the inside. I probably should have said it out loud, but I didn't. I didn't last three months either.

A few weeks into my stay at the Salvation Army, I learned that my house was being sold because obviously, I couldn't make the payments. My sister took on the monumental task of getting it ready to sell, including removing everything from the house I had lived in for over 15 years. I was embarrassed and ashamed, yet I pushed those heavy emotions way down as deep as I could. I didn't tell anybody.

One afternoon at the Salvation Army, a beautiful, dark skinned woman called me to her office and asked if I was okay. I told her I would be and then she asked a question that I'll never forget.

She said, "Do you know that you are wonderfully and fearfully made?"

I started crying. I sure didn't feel like it. Then she looked into my eyes and said she had a vision the night before, that I was walking outside with a box in my hand, alone.

Chad was released to a Salvation Army an hour away in Bridgeport and when we met he pulled a small container of ghb from his pocket. At first, I was angry but eventually I gave in and took a small sip. The staff at Salvation Army knew I was acting differently and said if I was honest with them, they would help me. I took a deep breath and admitted to my relapse. They removed me from the premises, handed me a small box of food and I was immediately homeless for the first time in my life. I never told anyone it was Chad who gave me the drug. I was too embarrassed, and I felt protective and responsible for him too.

Being handcuffed and sent back to the detention center sent thoughts of suicide through my brain. *Maybe I don't belong on this planet. Why do I hurt my family so badly, when I love them? What is wrong with me?*

There are no words to describe my pain, but isn't that in itself selfish? The pain took me to another level I had never experienced. I felt different occupying the same cell I was released from just a few months earlier. The fight was gone. I didn't feel like a person anymore.

Do you know that you are fearfully and wonderfully made?

What feelings does that evoke?

What parts of you are obviously wonderful?

Have you ever found yourself back in a place you never thought you'd go? (write your reflections on pages 112-113)

Jesus in Jail

I am familiar with stories in the Bible. Sunday school was part of my childhood and I spent many Sundays in church surrounded by people who loved me. Now I was in a prison cell. Again. Alone. There were women out in the day room watching tv and boisterously playing cards but I was finding it hard to breathe in and out. The best I could do was walk. Walk around the perimeter of the dull, cream colored walls. I walked around and around, and every other lap I forced myself to walk up and down the stairs that lined some of the walls. I stood on the top tier overlooking the entirety of my living condition and I wanted to throw up. Depression flooded my soul.

An elderly woman from a local church came in on Tuesdays and I finally went in to see what it was about. She had short, tightly curled blond hair, sprinkled with gray and a welcoming smile. I sat three chairs down from her and watched while she chatted with the girls. I learned she was Catholic as they started speaking about saints. Oh great she's going to try to convert me, a poor sinner, I thought. She started passing around something shaped like a playing card. I was handed one with a photo of St. Francis of Assisi on the front and the back was a prayer. I smiled and wondered how many of the women here have been to Assisi. I kept the fact that I had to myself.

The woman started talking about Jesus and how much He loved us and forgave us and that we needed to forgive ourselves. Then she turned directly to me.

"Do you know Jesus?" she asked. It felt like an odd and frankly, personal question to ask someone she just met. I told her that I didn't believe in saints, I knew that much.

She smiled and said, "That's okay, you don't have to."

I liked that she permitted me to think how I wanted.

"I am not comfortable with finding Jesus in jail. It sounds disgusting, almost as bad as committing a crime."

She smiled widely.

"Honey, just talk to him. This is where he has your undivided attention."

The hair on the back of my neck stood straight up. She was right. I wasn't going anywhere. I was suddenly flooded with a sense of peace.

This was the start of my deep spiritual journey. I had a foundation from childhood, but all of a sudden my days became filled with questioning, searching, reading, listening and wondering if just maybe the peace that I feel when I highlight and read scripture in Psalms before I went to bed was part of an energy source available to me at all times. Did I actually have the power to access peace whenever I wanted?

Spoiler alert: The answer was and still is a big Hell Yes!

Do you believe in a power bigger than yourself?

Do you have the freedom to form your own belief about God?

Can you access peace whenever you want? (write your reflections on pages 114-115)

Light and Dark

I was beginning to feel the power of being connected to God and other people. Letting others truly know me and accepting help was new. As a young girl, I was praised for being a fierce warrior, especially from my father. I wore that label proudly and it was easy for me to be strong when I was alone. I was alone in prison yet I knew there were people on the outside that were rooting for me.

It was a strange feeling to realize that nothing about me was very private anymore. It was also a strange feeling to know that people still loved me after I committed a crime. My brain couldn't comprehend it. My aunt MaryAnn said she would put money on my books to buy sneakers, so I could comfortably walk around the dayroom. She didn't have a lot of money and it was hard to accept her generosity.

When I told her that I was uncomfortable with it she said, "God gives me back double what I give so you're actually doing me a favor."

I will never forget those words. I have since said those words myself.

My sister came to visit me in Rhode Island, but I didn't want her to. My pattern of wanting to face pain alone continued. I didn't want her to see me at my absolute worst, dressed in an orange jumpsuit, handcuffed. The thought of exposing anyone in my family to this disgusting place was brutal. I didn't want them to experience any part of my criminal consequences.

My sister didn't care, she was coming anyway. How would I be able to look her in the eyes? I felt pain and love mixed with horrible guilt and shame.

When the officer came and escorted me to the bathroom for the customary strip search I began to cry. Both of my worlds were colliding and it was the most pain I'd felt in a long time. What the hell was I doing here? I reminded myself not to appear weak. The officer didn't say a word but when I started to walk out the door of iPod, the other women in my unit cheered me on.

"Good luck, it'll be fine, she just wants to know you're ok, don't be afraid, enjoy your sister."

This was only the second time I was allowed to leave my pod.

I was sitting on the metal stool staring at the glass with the phone attached to it when Tamara came around the corner. Pain, like I've never felt, enveloped my body and I couldn't stop crying. I was forced to face my reality at that moment.

I picked up the receiver and pushed the buttons 47510048. This allowed us to hear each other after she picked up the receiver on the other side. I can't remember a lot of what was said, but I do remember the way she made me feel. LOVED. ACCEPTED. WORTHY.

When the officer said our time was up I felt a panic. I didn't want to be left alone again. She saw something in me worth saving. We were in negotiations for a bit about who would walk away first. I think I was the one that left first. I didn't care about people seeing me cry anymore. Fuck it. This shit was sad. I was sad.

Do you have a friend or family member you trust?

Can you think of a time you experienced love, acceptance, and worthiness?

Are you carrying secrets that weigh you down?

Who is a person that will help you carry your load?

Why are you hiding? (write your reflections on pages 116-117)

Judgment Day

August 21st. My birthday. And my sentencing day, isn't that ironic? Birth day, judgment day. It's almost too much to comprehend. Being that it was my birthday, and I had already been incarcerated for 20 months, I had a glimmer of hope the judge would let me out with time served.

I was silent in the white, steel-barred windowed van, transporting us to the courtroom. I was the only female in the front row, and the rest of the seats were filled with shackled boys and men. I say boys because some of them looked so young. They somehow knew it was my sentencing day and I was unprepared for the positive words about how I would be okay, no matter the outcome. A van filled with fear, trauma, love, and kindness was a particularly interesting environment that deepened my need to connect with people who don't look like me.

I wish everybody could experience just a few of the poignant moments I had with black and brown men who were shackled in the several trips we took back and forth in that van to the courthouse. I cried with them and engaged in silly jokes. We exchanged hopes and dreams and provided positive encouragement when it was deemed appropriate and necessary.

There weren't as many smiles hanging in the air on sentencing day. Just nods, winks, and "You will be okay." Really, what else is there to say? Some of them were facing 20, 25, 33 years for non-violent drug conspiracy charges. Those are big numbers that are difficult to embrace. They call them football numbers.

When I got there my attorney said for me to brace for seven years. Seven years. 2,555 days in a cage.

As a first-time offender that felt overly excessive. All of it was too much to make sense of. It was hard to have my family there. The look in their eyes as I entered the courtroom shackled is a look I will never forget, and Mom looked the most afraid I had ever seen her in my life. I was causing her all that pain and it was destroying both of us. Oftentimes we don't realize the profound ripple effect our poor choices have on the ones we love until it's too late.

When the proceedings began, at first the prosecutor said nice things about me. How I didn't set out to be a drug dealer and how I had been burdened with health issues for most of my life. I was beginning to like him for a minute and then without skipping a beat he flipped and argued his case for sentencing me to 10 years in prison. I was horrified.

The judge gave me 5 years.

When I got back to the van I was crying and pissed. The CO's were playing a song by Akon in the van on the way back to the detention center.

"I got locked up, they won't let me out," the song boomed.

I guess it was appropriate.

What were some of the poor choices you made that affected others?

Do you think about that in your current interactions with people? (write your reflections on pages 118-119)

Change of Plans

For my sentencing, the judge said I would be going to a camp in California. My mother was already making arrangements to visit me when plans changed and I was called to get on the bus going to Texas. FMC Carswell was a medical facility and once sentenced, the BOP (Bureau of Prisons) can send you anywhere they want. I didn't know anything about the maximum security prison when I arrived and I was afraid. I went to the only source I had immediate access to and said a prayer.

I was beginning to find my own understanding of who God was, and I established an intimate relationship with the one who provides peace amongst chaos. Upon arrival, the 15 women or so that came with me from Oklahoma (the transfer center I went to after Rhode Island) were each sizing everyone up. I was too.

Amber was kind and funny and silly, but her friend Brenda, who was a strikingly beautiful brunette, seemed annoyed by me. Never a smile or a glance in my direction.

As Amber began to include me in her conversations Brenda seemed to get increasingly irritated, so I held back. I was agitated and hungry and in shock that I wasn't going to a minimum security camp in California. Those fears started to subside when all of a sudden, two women began singing gospel so simply and beautifully. I had never been exposed to gospel, didn't know the songs at all but it began to soothe me. My heart felt warm and peaceful when they sang and I didn't want them to stop.

"Take Me to the King", I later learned, was the name of the first song they sang. My heart stirred in a deep way that had never in my lifetime been stirred before. Now on the surface you would think that a bunch of convicts listening or singing to a gospel song would be ridiculous, even offensive. *Take me to the King* as we were waiting to go to our cell. I stopped the chatter in my head and opened my heart and just listened. Tears ran down my cheeks. The echo within the walls was quite astounding which made them sing even louder and with more conviction. If I could have lived in that moment for the remaining time of my sentence I would have.

Of course, that would not be the case, but what that moment did was create a voracious appetite to experience that feeling again. I decided then that I would need to learn more about gospel music.

Now, whenever I'm feeling anxious or heavy I play my gospel music and it soothes my soul. I have access to that peace whenever I need it.

Write about a time that a song or a certain kind of music touched you deeply.

Are you in touch with yourself enough to make choices that will help you?
(write your reflections on pages 120-121)

Inauthentic

I have a million stories about my time in prison, but the purpose of our time together here is to work through our most transformational moments so I need to tell you about the biggest and most painful experience.

I got kicked out of RDAP - Two times! This expulsion required me to do another whole year in prison. RDAP is the Residential Drug Program in federal prison. It still is the season in my life that carries the most anger, the place I need to extract forgiveness for and make peace with the months that broke me in half.

I'm not sure how to describe this season in my life because my feelings around it keep evolving, the more inner work I do. I didn't know it was possible for my body to produce hatred like they provoked. I wanted revenge in the worst way and that's a new feeling for me as well. I've been surprised by the range of uncomfortable emotions RDAP brought out in me. They took who I thought I was, flipped it upside down, and then stomped on it day after day. Over and over. For months.... wearing Gucci stilettos. Yes, the director was into fashion.

I learned about two words in this program. Shame and Authentic. The first time they kicked me out, they said I was associating with a known compound drug dealer.

She was my previous bunky and I stopped to tell her how RDAP was going when she asked. That's all it took.

Everyone in Carswell told me not to do the program because they said I wouldn't graduate. The program had a reputation for being abusive and difficult at best. They expected each of us in the program to tell on each other as a way to establish accountability and responsibility. I tried to give the program the benefit of the doubt since I knew I had work to do on myself, but we were all getting crushed, some of us beyond repair.

I did learn a lot about my people-pleasing tendencies and my inability to be honest about my feelings regardless if they hurt someone. The counselors incessantly exposed our pain, but they broke us, left us there, and then laughed at us. They hurt women. They hurt me. They broke off the identity of masks I had carried (which in itself was necessary) but left me broken and then kicked me out because they said I wasn't authentic.

The director also said she was glad I couldn't have children because I would have made a terrible mother. Yes. She said those words to me as she stood up and grabbed her Louis Vuitton bag. I was devastated. *Another message that something was wrong with me.* On my way back to my old unit, carrying my few belongings, I stopped to observe the jets flying above. I was as smart as those pilots, I knew it. So what was my problem?

Write about the last time you were furious.

Did your anger surprise you?

Have you been able to let that go?

Have you ever felt like something was wrong with you? (write your reflections on pages 122-123)

Acceptance

A year was a long time for me to be on an extended and unexpected time-out. Another punishment of sorts, beyond the original harsh sentence. I'd had it in my mind that I would be redeemed on a certain date but that was no longer the case. Another year in prison!!

This extra time sent me into an emotional spiral. I couldn't get my grounding on what was happening to my life, so I ran. No, I didn't try to escape. :) I ran on the track outside. Around and around, every chance I got.

Have you ever cried and ran at the same time? It's sad and difficult and a few times the ridiculousness of it all made me break out in crazy laughter. Snot, tears, anger and laughter all rolled up together. "What the hell is happening" was the name of the road that traveled from my head to my heart and then back again on a regular basis. I sincerely didn't understand all of the contradictions.

I worked during the day on landscaping duty. My landscape boss was a kind man with dark brown eyes. He barely said two words to anyone so when I told him, dripping with shame, that I was kicked out of the program he said more words to me than the culmination of all his words put together, the whole time I've worked for him.

"Laschober," he said. "Maybe they've never had anyone like you in their program before. Stay out of trouble, keep your head down, and then get the hell out of here. AND DON'T COME BACK."

His words were beautiful to my soul. He didn't shame me. I felt human again and a little like my old self, like he saw something in me that my sister did. I took his words to heart and mustered up all the acceptance I could. I accepted where I was as if my soul chose to be here and embraced every minute of this time in a Texas prison as a learning opportunity. I purposefully shifted my perception, over and over again, sometimes twenty times a day.

When was the last time you purposefully shifted your perception?

Do you need to get into acceptance about something right now? (write your reflections on pages 124-125)

A Deeper Understanding

For the next year in prison, I created a routine for myself. I worked, worked out, went to church, made greeting cards to sell for commissary, and ran around the track. I got up at 6 am, went to the chow hall for "not toasted" toast, bran cereal resembling cardboard and if it were a special day, the milk would not be curdled and I would get a banana. Then I'd walk the long road to Facilities, in my extra heavy, black work boots. We'd go through security, with food to cook in the only microwave there was and plan the work day.

Most days were spent outside, bent over flower beds, weeding, planting, and watering with large, heavy buckets. One day as I watered around newly transplanted flowers, talking to God in my head, a blue, iridescent winged dragonfly perched on a stick inches from where I was working. He stayed there most of the day and came back the next.

After several days of noticing my beautiful, perfect, fluttery friend, I felt God speak to me deep in my soul. I knew it was God by the way I felt so peaceful in my heart. The words I heard rang true to me: *This is what praying without ceasing means. You can talk to me all day, every day, about everything.*

I breathed in His message to remind me when I felt anxious and it helped. I made it a point to talk to God in the flowers for the rest of my stay. I had a lot of things to say, a lot of questions that I needed answered. And you know what? He listened. I started realizing that I was really talking to myself, that God's spirit lives inside of me. God is the best version of Kristy. The closest version to the original human He created.

This brought me a lot of comfort and grew my authenticity. Believing that God was living inside of me helped me treat myself better. I even started to love myself in a deep way. I began paying attention to everything about me. I was discovering the light and dark parts of me without judgment. I embraced all of myself and it was incredible.

Have you ever had a spiritual experience?

Could the best version of yourself be considered God?

How did you get through an excruciating experience?

Do you know that you are a bad-ass? (write your reflections on pages 126-127)

Another Chance

I was laying on the top bunk staring at the ceiling, which was not far from my face. I couldn't sleep. So many thoughts were running through my head. It was eerily quiet, even though the light, as usual, was so bright. I knew I had to sleep, it would be my last night in prison. I rolled over on my side and cringed at that horrible plastic crinkle sound. It had become like nails on a chalkboard. I must have drifted off, because I woke up to my other bunky attempting to be quiet as she wrestled through her locker, getting dressed for her laundry job. Four of us were in that tiny cell.

Our eyes met, and she whispered, "Today's the day Laschober."

I smiled. I was going to miss Kristen. My heart hurt knowing that this day would never come for her. She would never see the outside of the prison walls. I jumped down from the top bunk and quietly opened my locker. I already had my belongings set aside, strategically planning on who I was going to give what to.

Kristen was going to get most of my art supplies and art magazines. She was my crafty friend and so unimaginably talented. I had planned to give my work boots to Teresa, they weren't her size but I knew she could sell them for $80 worth of commissary food. Item by item, I gave it all away except for my alarm clock, my gray sweatpants and one pink lipliner. Keeping something pretty for my lips brought me joy.

Then I heard it, my name was called on the loudspeaker. I had been waiting for that sound for nearly five excruciatingly long years. As I slowly walked out the front door, nearing the barbed wire, I heard my name called again. It was Teresa, I recognized her voice. She was in the middle of her 14th year of a 27 year drug sentence.

I turned around to say goodbye one last time and the officer scoffed and said, "I knew it. You'll be back, Laschober. Everyone that turns around comes back."

I hated Mr. Penishead. His shiny badge said Mr. Butler but we called this mean, angry, bald, white man Penishead. Why did he have to be such a jerk? I would prove him wrong.

A small, unassuming car was waiting out front to pick me up. Girls from the minimum security camp were allowed to transport people to the airport. They asked if I liked Chris Brown and when I said yes, they blasted his song PARTY, playing it as loud as possible. All four windows were rolled down and the wind in my hair felt delicious. I closed my eyes trying to imagine my future and even though tears rolled down my face, I had peace in my heart because I knew God lived inside of me and I knew that He would never leave me. I also had the distinct impression that He was badass and wanted a lot of cool things for me. I trusted both of us and it was such a beautiful, new feeling. The ladies dropped me off in front of the airport and I walked through the terminal, for the first time in my life, without any luggage, and a crystal clear, clean slate in front of me.

Write about a time you were embarking on a new chapter of your life.

Was it what you expected? (write your reflections on pages 128-129)

Courage Required

There is only one halfway house in the entire state of Oregon, and it happens to be minutes away from my family. This was a giant blessing. I wrote in my journal every day and each morning on the top of the page I wrote the same phrase, "Help me be of service and help me be a light in someone's life."

This declaration helped me realize that I still had something valuable to give. I had lost all my possessions except a few things, and I was battling to remember my worthiness. Writing was beginning to be my sacred place where I could process my feelings and let some of the crazy out of my head. I started writing a few months before I left prison and it was surprisingly easy for me to carry on the habit to the halfway house.

The staff was kinder than the CO's in prison but there was still an edge of hyper-authority to some of them. I kept hearing how mean my PO Aimee was, so I wasn't looking forward to meeting her. To my relief, I found that not to be true. Aimee was kind and funny, and treated me with respect. How refreshing. We were off to a good start.

After a short time, I was able to get a pass for various reasons. To visit my mother, go to church, a 12-step meeting, and eventually look for a job. I learned the bus route and looked forward to riding the bus on my own into town. My mom struggled with me taking the bus. She would have much rather driven me everywhere I needed to go.

Sometimes, I forget how hard this whole experience has been for her. What would it be like to have your daughter caught up in a sensationalized media storm involving prison, addiction, and a catholic priest? My mom loved me and she cared about what other people thought, as do most of us. Addiction is such a selfish son-of-a-bitch that destroys every lovely thing.

My sister bought me a phone on her family plan and I found a job at a downtown hotel. It was perfect for me. I was growing, little by little, tip-toeing into discovering the best version of myself. I carried an unusual boldness that complimented my gratitude and family support. I felt an extreme sense of urgency to be courageous and do good. I felt unstoppable.

Has your life ever been in a holding pattern?

What did you do in the waiting?

Do you have a sense of urgency to be courageous? (write your reflections on pages 130-131)

Re-Entering

The case manager at the halfway house recommended that I go to re-entry court. He said that once completed I would be eligible for a year off of my probation. Hmmmm, I've heard that before. I wasn't sure if I could trust that same carrot people in the criminal punishment system liked to dangle.

I finally decided to at least check it out because I had been given five years probation and from everything I've heard, being on probation causes multiple barriers to success. I'm glad I took another risk and went to re-entry court.

Let me describe the scene for you: Picture a conference room with long tables shaped in a circle. At those tables were judges, probation officers, defense attorneys, prosecutors, drug and alcohol counselors, community members, and whoever else wanted to show up. Federal Judge Ann Aiken was at the helm and she was dressed in nice clothes like you'd see on the racks at Chicos. It was intense.

Once accepted into the program, the requirement was attendance once a month for twelve months with clean UA's (urine analysis). Easy enough, I thought. One Friday a month, we would meet in the room and talk about how our month was. There were generally around twelve federal inmates, mostly men who were recently released, and Ann was there to provide help and resources to all of us. At first, it was overwhelming and mind blowing - receiving help from the same authority figure who put most of us in prison for years and years.

My sentencing judge was in Connecticut so I didn't have that familiar history to deal with. Ann listened to each of us disclose our fears, and barriers to getting a driver's license, child care, and emotional counseling. The list of what people re-entering back into society needed was extensive. Ann recommended books, connected people to resources, and listened. And when I say she listened, I mean Ann actively listened.

I was witnessing a miracle. People who had been crushed by authority were being heard and engaged with. They were seen as whole, beautiful beings with massive amounts of potential. Ann seemed to really care. They all did. It was not easy sharing in front of everyone around the table about what was on my mind. But I did and each time it got easier. Re-entry court was where I practiced being my true and authentic self, in front of people, for the first time in my life and it was scary as hell.

But they believed in me and expected nothing in return. I was starting to really believe in myself and working at shedding shame and guilt. I also needed help letting go of Chad, the person I went to prison with. Chad got out before me because he completed RDAP, which was a blessing for me because he relapsed and I wasn't around to relapse with him. He couldn't stop.

I had guilt that I was doing so well and he wasn't. I felt guilty for moving forward while he was still stuck. The judge helped me through that. The judge helped all of us who were willing to receive her help, push past shame, isolation, and manipulation. She was helping us re-enter society as healthy as possible.

What makes it hard for you to be completely authentic in front of others?

In what one area can you begin being authentic?

Who is your authentic self?

Which person in your life knows you the best? (write your reflections on pages 132-133)

Shame Obliterated

During one of our sessions, the judge asked why I wasn't in college. I didn't know what to say. The truth was, I was 52 years old and found it hard to not think I passed my opportunity for college a long time ago. I didn't even know what I wanted to do. What career would I choose?

I know I am smart. I also know that I have never tried very hard in school. I always achieved because other people wanted me to, but I didn't have the necessary intrinsic determination to succeed. I gave away all my true power and floated through my life like a balloon let go into the sky, getting caught on tree branches and telephone wires every so often.

I began thinking about college and decided to give it a try. One sunny day I made the move and walked up the steps of the community college. My self-talk was brutal but finally, I took my damn power back and said out loud to myself, "Kristy, you lived in a tiny cell with three convicted criminals! You can open this door and sign up for college!"

I have to admit, that contrast between what I'd already been through and what I had ahead of me left a permanent smile on my face for the afternoon. Why are we so afraid of the unknown? Why am I so ashamed of my mistakes when they've brought me to where I am today?

When I sat down in front of the young lady that would be helping me fill out financial aid papers, I was grateful for her kind and welcoming demeanor. She asked me questions and I gave her answers. Everything was going great until she asked me about a gap in my home addresses. There it was. I knew it was coming. I swallowed and took a deep cleansing breath before I said, "I actually was in federal prison for those years. I had five different addresses so I wasn't sure what to list on the application."

My knees were shaking. There were a hundred possibilities for responses and she chose one that would set me on a trajectory of transparency and courage for the rest of my life.

"Oh my gosh, you are incredible," she exclaimed. "This is going to be great. I am so excited for you".

Tears run down my face as I write this because it's still so emotional. This woman I just met, single-handedly obliterated more of my shame.

Write about a time you persevered through something scary.

Did somebody unexpectedly help you through it? (write your reflections on pages 134-135)

Destined for Happiness

Each day of my new life felt magical. All rolled into one day were the feelings of fear, gratitude, excitement, trepidation, and curiosity. I had the distinct feeling that I was destined to be happy if I only believed I would be. I met a variety of different women who encouraged my transparency and listened to my stories. They were genuinely happy to support and share in my successes. All of these relationships provided a deep love that I had never experienced.

My mother, sister, and I were healing, sharing, and speaking honestly about our emotions. My sister was my ride-or-die confidant who helped me make sense of family triggers so that I could move past pain more quickly and with compassion for myself and everyone else.

Only one of my relationships still had unwanted tension and I was ready to do something about it.

My step mom Diane and I had a long, tumultuous history. I felt a strong loyalty to my mother and was uncomfortable with the attention my father lavished on Diane. She had reasons not to care for me too much either. I wasn't easy and our personalities clashed. She was a free spirit and I envied her freedom. I would get so mad that she could be late, make silly mistakes, and act in ways my family used to deem "inappropriate." I didn't understand why it was okay now.

Towards the end of my prison stay, Diane sent me a letter, describing all the exotic traveling she had been doing. Along with the letter, she sent a hardcover picture book that displayed vibrant images of the top places to travel all over the world. I vacillated between longing curiosity and irritated anger.

"Why would she send me a letter bragging about her travels when I'm locked up hundreds of miles away?" I had confided my dilemma with a younger girl named Lisa, who I met in RDAP and she posed a unique question that set me on a path of potential freedom.

"I think you're jealous. I think you wish you were as free as she is. She knows you love to travel so maybe that letter and book were an attempt to connect with you. Maybe you should start a new relationship with her now that your dad is gone. Maybe you can be free like Diane."

I remembered that day in prison when Lisa's words gave me permission to re-frame my entire attitude and put the story I'd been telling myself away. Perhaps there was some truth to all of it. Perhaps I was jealous. Maybe Diane didn't know how painful the letter was to read while I was locked away in hell. How could she know if she'd never experienced being incarcerated?

I was no longer comfortable with the very long history I had of not liking her. I couldn't get the possibility of freedom and forgiveness out of my mind. How cool would it be to put everything from the past, in the past and start fresh.

I longed to begin a new relationship in 2017 without bringing all the baggage from 1987. I figured if I'm going to roam around in the world as a loving, trusting, compassionate type of person, I'd have to clean up this relationship with Diane.

And so I did. Because she was also willing to have a current relationship with me, we got to know each other on a new level. Today I have a loving, respectful relationship with the woman I was once jealous of. We just got back from an amazing trip to South Africa.

What relationship do you have that brings tension?

Have you tried to start over and engage in a current relationship?

Can you let the past hurts of that relationship go? (write your reflections on pages 136-137)

Smarty Pants

My college journey was the best thing that I could have done for my growth in every single area. Learning was more layered than I expected and even though I hadn't done math in 30 years, I just went for it. My age and maturity allowed me to be comfortable with asking for help, and asking lots of questions whenever I didn't understand the assignment. I was advised to get a tutor for math and on the first day we met, this young boy of 16 years introduced himself as Chad. Can you believe it?

It took me a minute to let the wave of irony crash over me. I smiled at God because I'm learning that He has a great sense of humor. Tutor Chad was smart beyond his years. I was his first college student so between the two of us, success was inevitable. He wanted to do well for me and I wanted to do well for both of us. Ten weeks of working with Tutor Chad made that name I used to love so much have a different connotation. Every time I said his name my heart twinged and I realized God was healing me with humor.

God's always working inside of me, sometimes it's just more obvious than others. Tutor Chad helped me prepare for my first exam and I was ready, although scared to death. I wanted a good grade, as I was still equating success with achievement. I thought I did okay and was pretty sure I passed when the professor handed me my exam upside down while giving me a funny look. Fear and doubt struck hard so I immediately lowered my standard.

"I just want a C," I thought.

When I slowly turned my exam over, I couldn't believe what I saw.

Was this a joke? Am I being punked? Without saying a word to any of my classmates I looked around the room as tears started to spill from my eyes. I wanted to get on the table and scream. "NO WAY!! I got an A. 100%. I KNEW I WAS SMART!"

I could barely contain myself. I wanted to hug someone but I didn't know anyone in the class like that. No one else seemed too excited and I didn't want to brag but this was the best thing that had happened to me in a very long time.

Over the next few years, including my two years at the university, I continued to excel in school. Eventually graduating summa cum laude with a BS in Innovation and Leadership. Out of all the exams I took, that first one was still the most impactful. The crazy joy I felt lasted days and carried over into every other part of my life. Maybe I wasn't broken. Maybe there wasn't anything wrong with me after all. Maybe, who I was was perfect - and perfectly flawed - all along. Maybe the journey ahead of me was to get back to myself.

Write about a time you were so excited and proud of yourself.

What were the emotions you felt?

Do you still take time to acknowledge your successes? (write your reflections on pages 138-139)

Letting Go

It had been a year since I'd been out of prison and I decided to go back to California for a visit. I was waiting in the parking lot of the hotel for Chad to come pick me up and I couldn't stop crying. It was so strange.

Here we were both back in San Clemente for the first time in almost six years. I was bodily and emotionally sober and sobbing uncontrollably. I ran quickly inside to the lobby to grab some tissue but there wasn't any and then I noticed his dad's green BMW pulled into the driveway. I tried to pull it together by whispering, "God help me, please give me strength!" while taking the deepest breath I could possibly take.

Chad got out of the car and we didn't even look at each other, we just fell into the familiar, comfortable embrace that had been a long time coming. My arms reached around closer than I remembered - he is skinny. I sobbed and didn't say a word. He told me that it was going to be okay, but I couldn't believe him.

How the hell did we get to this moment? What does our future look like? Will he be able to stay sober? Will he live a happy life? Will the next time I see him be at his funeral? What can I say to him that I haven't already said a thousand times to bring him peace and contentment? Will I find this kind of love again without all the toxicity that comes with this particular beautiful person? Questions raced through my mind.

In my heart, I knew those questions could not be answered. Perhaps they will be revealed eventually somewhere in the future and my deep prayer is that I will be courageous and grounded and peaceful enough to handle when they come about.

This is a new, scary, and wonderful way to go through life as a happy person. I don't have to have all the answers figured out. I just have to show up as my best, highest, most loving self. I am finding that's usually where the magic happens. It gives space for others to grow in their own personal journey too.

I was in San Clemente to get some of my things for my old house. Getting out of the car in front of the house that Chad and I had fled from all those years ago was surreal. It looked the same. The sun was shining and the deep blue ocean presented a beautiful California day like I had been used to. It was so far from the beige walls of the prison that had felt like an eternity.

Chad had organized the few belongings I had left in the garage and I was surprised to read some of the labels. My box of favorite Christmas ornaments, pictures of my trip to Europe in 1987, and my champagne-colored quilted bedspread. I saw the lucite lamp I loved so much and almost burst into tears. Chad and I had bought it together in Palm Springs.

I needed to go slow and absorb these memories that were rushing back at me. I felt his nervousness which made me try to be more chill and a little silly. As I looked around the rest of the garage he made the first of many of the same comments, "If there is anything you see that you want, please take it."

His softness and love made me cry again. So much hurt and pain and damage and regret filled the air. I decided to take the plunge and walk into the house. As I stepped through the door, I realized I had never been inside sober. The orange, hi-gloss kitchen cabinets complemented the white sparkle countertop. It was beautiful. I felt like I died and was floating above myself, reliving my life many years ago, trying to recognize that rebellious, troubled, lost woman that spent so much time here. My heart ached for her.

Have you ever felt the weight of letting go of the past?

What actions did you take to move forward? (write your reflections on pages 140-141)

Shawshank Moments

Every week I spoke to one of my old bunkies, Lorraine. She had been deported to Canada before I was released while her family still lived in the States. We talked about our vivid nightmares of being sent back to prison and the different ways we were adjusting to life outside of the walls. We reminisced about the terrifying conditions in which we first met.

That day I was brought to a cell on the second floor in unit one north at Carswell, a federal prison known as the "Hospital of Horrors." It's true. Google it.

When Lorraine looked up from reading her book to greet me, I thought, "She looks normal, I wonder what she's in here for?"

Even though I was a prisoner myself I still had preconceived ideas about what an incarcerated woman looked like. Lorraine was kind and showed me which locker was mine, although I didn't have anything to put in it yet. Lorraine gave me shampoo, conditioner, lotion and food. I can't remember exactly what kind of food because I was still shell-shocked from my new living arrangement. She made sure I had everything I needed to feel comfortable in a 6x8 foot cell along with two other inmates, one of which was a ferocious bully.

Lorraine and I started a deep friendship birthed from pain, scarcity, and fear. We were at our lowest and away from anyone who loved us. For many months we talked about what we would do if we were free again, about how nice it would be to hear waves crashing and feel sand under our feet. How when we got out we would do something to make a difference.

Fast forward two years since we said our last tearful goodbyes, and we met again.
On a beach.
In Cozumel, Mexico.

We were hearing waves crashing and feeling sand under our feet – as completely different women.

We both had worked our asses off to get to this spot. Amongst everything else we accomplished, we had the same, short term goal – to meet on a beach in Mexico. We ate fresh seafood, snorkeled in bright blue, crystal clear water and got massages on the beach. We were free and fully responsible for how we lived out the rest of our lives.

Life for me now is about connection and empathy and sharing stories. Hope is what keeps all of us going, especially women in prison. I had to dig and claw my way to grasp at any ounce of hope I could find.

It took effort to have hope because of the flood of frightening stories I heard about getting out of prison. I heard over and over how hard it was going to be and how most people don't succeed. A 70% recidivism rate is no joke. Everyone says that once you're in the system, you'll never get out. But I have found this to be objective at best. Everyone thinks that incarceration and addiction put you at a disadvantage, but I have found otherwise.

All of my experiences have prepared me to walk firmly into my purpose and use those transferable skills to my advantage. It's a matter of believing in myself and believing that I have developed unique skills that others in my community may not have had to. I had to be humble and ask for help, and in doing so I got help from every corner of my community. Did I have to work hard? YES. Did I have to be responsible for my actions and follow the rules? Yes. Did I have to do things that I was afraid of? Oh Hell Yes! Everyday!

> *Write about a trip you went on with a friend. What was most memorable?*
>
> *Who are your most beautiful connections with?*
>
> *Are you taking full responsibility for how your life is going?* (write your reflections on pages 142-143)

Dark and Light are Good

One of the benefits of going through something painfully difficult is obtaining a deep understanding that you can be stretched beyond what you ever thought was possible. I would guess that I was probably living at 40% of what I was capable of. I think a lot of us have no idea what 100% capacity looks like. How about 75%? Most people probably have no idea the magnitude of what they can create/achieve/endure when they no longer hide different aspects of themselves.

Once I started to embrace my dark and light side and actually let those characteristics out in the sunlight to play with each other, life became like a beautiful amusement park, with long roller coaster rides and churros. It's the new journey of knowing, trusting and loving ourselves deeply. When you know you're doing your best and saying yes rather than dimming your light and shrinking in fear, you simply don't judge yourself anymore. Achievement and success look different for everybody and the great thing is that we get to decide what it is for us. We get to listen to our gut and trust ourselves.

Our soul wants us to be bold and brave, even when we don't think we're ready. That's where the trust comes in. When you are connected to yourself, you trust all the parts of you. I only started living this way after I was released from prison. That's the gift of having all your secrets aired out to the world.

One morning I was on Twitter and out of nowhere, I received a personal tweet from a gentleman at Stanford. In his tweet, he wrote that he just helped pass a bill in the state of Washington which would remove the criminal history box from all college applications. He said he noticed that I was incarcerated as was he, and that the experience was so amazing he wanted other formerly incarcerated people to experience it as well. Then he asked the question: *Do you want to pass the bill in Oregon?*

Me? Pass a law?

"OKAY."

I said Yes! I trusted myself. I trusted Noel Vest. I wasn't afraid to ask for help or reach out to any of my professors. I knew a couple of judges that could probably help me answer some of my questions and I remember the feeling of getting 100% on my very first test. From then on the aching question of *"wonder what else I am capable of"* stayed with me. It took two years of meetings and finding other justice-impacted people in Oregon. We met with senators and house of representatives and even went to the state capital before covid shut everything down. I breathed in the energy and grandness of it all, so different from the trauma of a prison cell.

I was walking around government officials in a nice suit and briefcase, rather than wearing a khaki uniform, shackled. It made me feel like I grabbed some of my power back from the bureau of prisons. We submitted written and oral testimony over zoom a couple of times and it was powerful.

The best part? The bill passed and the governor signed it in 2021. What a feeling!

What are some of the things stirring in your heart and soul, you have yet to address?

What stops you from saying yes?

What does achievement and success look like to you? (write your reflections on pages 144-145)

Using my voice

When I was in prison I had no idea that people were outside of the walls fighting for justice. That they were fighting for clemency, for humane treatment, and advocating for the abolishment of unusually harsh sentences. I stayed off social media for the first 18 months out of prison because I wasn't prepared to face the people I abruptly left in California, and I was busy in school.

Once I opened the door to Facebook, Instagram, and Twitter, my world got massive. I met amazing people who had been paving the way to speak about mass incarceration and who are now involved in a plethora of transformational activities all over the country. I experienced encouragement from people I had never met but who were also impacted by the criminal punishment system, and I liked it.

On the first page of one of my first text books, by Austin Kleon, it read, "Shout what you have to say from the rooftops, and the people that need to hear you will hear you."

That statement jumped out at me and I took it as permission to keep sharing my story. I shared my story in church groups, on various panels, and in intimate settings. I shared my story at a Women's Leadership Conference, where my friend Lindsay and I spoke on the topic of Disrupting Leadership Culture. Lindsay was a new friend who treated me with more respect and love than I yet had for myself. We were so different, I wondered why she liked me so much.

People are so complex and beautiful. People that hear your story and then partner up with you in various ways can be a powerful force. We are meant to do life together. Not separate. Not alone. Not hidden. Not fear-based. We are meant to connect through all of our layered experiences. We each have so many parts of ourselves that are complemented by people who don't look like us. The insides of how we connect are merged through various cultures and I found that out because of all the women I engaged with in prison. I was surprised by how much I had in common with people who didn't look like me. Prison is a melting pot of cultures, socio economic backgrounds, environments, neighborhoods, and family dynamics.

Now that I am out, I still gravitate to people who don't look like me. I'm drawn to different cultures and traditions, and I love that I belong.

How diverse is your friend circle?

Do you have friends in different cultures?

What interests you about other cultures? (write your reflections on pages 146-147)

Mentorship

The power of mentorship is astounding. I had no idea how much a mentor could help me navigate the life I am meant to live. Besides my mother and sister, I've had a few women mentors since being released from prison. Each of them brings a different aspect of success to my future.

Gina was introduced to me by a friend I knew from my past. While I was still in prison I asked him if he knew of a woman that could mentor me when I got out. That's when I met Gina. She guided me through the vast array of emotions I was experiencing and reminded me that crying was simply an emotion, like laughing. She encouraged me to keep my perspective positive and open to new adventures.

Judge Ann Aiken was a mentor that helped bridge my incarceration experience over to professionalism and opportunities. Every chance she could, Ann included me in professional settings and scooped me into her speaking opportunities. She even introduced me as her "dear friend." Those two words still have a huge impact on the way I see myself. She was my judge. I was the offender. Now we are *dear friends*. We talk on the phone and she asks for my advice. Sometimes, actually oftentimes, I stop and pay attention to these powerful interactions and let the moments seep into my soul. Reminding myself that I belong everywhere and I can give that same love and attention to others. Words matter.

My friend Lindsay, who I spoke about earlier, has walked alongside my journey since we first met, soon after I was released from prison. She also included me in many opportunities and I often wondered why she did. In fact, I said to her once "Lindsay, please don't feel obligated to include me in everything, I'm just a student." I'll never forget the words she replied with. She said that I was on my way to doing great things and that she was going to take advantage of every moment with me. Somehow I believed her. She saw something in me that I hadn't seen in myself yet.

My friend Jenna had recently lost her mother due to a young man driving recklessly on drugs. Her mother was killed when the man ran a red light and fled the scene. Jenna's mom had worked hard her whole life to retire, and shortly after she did, she was taken from her family in a blink.

Eerily, that young man had the same sentencing date I did. A different year, but the same date. My heart sank as I realized that could have been me. There were several times when I could have been responsible for hurting someone else. Jenna and I talked a lot about each other's experience in the wake of deep tragedy.

Each time I struggled with abandoning myself and what I had learned, to please my mother, I went to Jenna. She wished her mother was still alive and I trusted what she said about how to proceed in unchartered territory of disappointing someone I loved to pursue my needs. I'll never forget what Jenna said to me in one of my struggles to choose what to do. We were on a walk and I told her I was going to compromise something.

She stopped and looked me in the eye and said, "What? You are considering not being true to yourself so you don't disappoint your mother? You are going to abandon your healing journey after it has taken you to where you are now? Are you sure you want to do that Kristy?"

Sometimes, actually, a lot of times in the quest of becoming authentic, our bravery is fueled by others. Others that have gone before us or those who are walking beside us and only want us to succeed. I am so grateful for the people God placed in my path.

Finding men or women outside of your family that supports you in your success is something very special. Actually, it's more than special. It's critical.

Do you have a mentor?

Are you a mentor to someone else?

What steps could you take to find a mentor? (write your reflections on pages 148-149)

The Freedom Exchange Project Conversations

I love having conversations with people about their life. I'm always hungry to hear how they've been able to pull themselves out of a gut-wrenching situation and begin the process of healing. I can see the sparkle of discovery in their eyes. It's familiar to me. There's a type of freedom that comes out of various shades of darkness. Sometimes the darkness lasts a day, sometimes much longer, but I can say for certain that we all have the ability to bring light into the darkness so that it dissipates quicker, which is a power I never knew I had. Opening up to safe people and being honest and compassionate with myself is the definition of freedom.

My own healing journey was sparked out of a desire to share my truth, no matter how ugly it used to feel. I say "used to" because I'm realizing that my past makes me human, not ugly or bad. Many of us are walking around with similar pasts but most of us aren't talking about it.

When we disown parts of ourselves, we judge the same parts in others. The more we hear about the humanity of others, our judgment dissipates and we become connected to others.

I started The Freedom Exchange Project because I wanted to challenge people's biases and amplify the incredible voices of others who have risen out of the fire. Allison was one of the first women I met coming out of prison. I didn't learn until later that her father was in federal prison and he stayed hidden in his shame. He never talked about it and told her not to. Allison and I were both system-impacted, coming from different experiences with unique insights. Before we knew what we were doing, we created a Facebook Live following and had hour-long conversations with people who had been in prison. I wanted the world to hear and see real-life people who had been locked in cages, sometimes for many years.

I felt like I had this special insight into what kind of people were in prison. It's different than everyone imagines. We are them and they are us. We are the same, whether you like it or not. When our guests shared about who they were at 12 years old, how they did in school, what their neighborhood was like, who their friends were, and what kind of traumatic events happened to them, our audience began to relate and express compassion. We continue to hope that these stories translate to awareness and action, and of course, connection.

What are some of the biases you have?

Who do you direct your biggest judgment toward?

What part of your disowned self are you judging? (write your reflections on pages 150-151)

I'M A COMPLEX HUMAN - THE JOURNEY CONTINUES

Maya Angelou and Brene' Brown are two of my heart heroes. Way back in 1973, Maya said, "You are only free when you realize you belong no place—you belong every place—no place at all. The price is high. The reward is great."

Brene interprets this wholehearted statement by saying, "We confuse belonging with fitting in, but the truth is that belonging is just in our heart, and when we belong to ourselves and believe in ourselves above all else, we belong everywhere and nowhere."

For me, writing creates belonging. Writing connects me to myself in such a thoughtful way. It's a sacred time of discovery that I lovingly carve out so that I don't get lost again. I am not afraid anymore about what I will find deep inside me. I smile a lot. I don't judge others and if I do, I go inward and find out why. I laugh at my silliness in attempting to stop eating so many sweets. I cry at the thought of all the moments I wasn't very nice to myself. I am a force. I am powerful and I am not ashamed of anything anymore. That's such a big statement that took me a long time to embrace. I am human and I do human things like say stupid stuff or cram too much into one day or binge watch a tv show or look for my next vacation spot while I'm already on vacation.

You are human too. All the little intricacies that make up who you are is beautiful and should be celebrated. I've learned that the people who want you to change are not comfortable in their own skin. They haven't done the inner work like you are in the process of doing. They need others around them to act in a specific way so that they are comfortable and that's NOT your job. Your job is to discover who you were born as. There is only one of you on the whole planet so of course you will not be for everybody. Don't expect to be.

As you do your work, past relationships and old conversations won't fit very well anymore, and that's okay. As you continue to excavate all of who you are, I can promise you this ... The people who step into your life to celebrate you oftentimes are people you wouldn't expect. They come from all cultures, work in various professions, are on a different side of your political persuasion, and may not dress like you. That's why it's so important to be open and curious. If you find yourself judging someone, write about it in your journal. It's a human trait that's ripe for discovering what you are judging about yourself. I mention this a few times because this is where freedom is.

Thank you for going on this journey with me. It's not easy being fully transparent. But don't we all deserve to be free?

What have I discovered about myself?

What perceived, shameful experiences can I use to catapult me to greatness?

What do I have to offer that other people around me don't?

Who can I call to ask them to walk on this new vulnerable path with me?

Who is my most free friend?

What makes them so free?

How can I lean into freedom more? (write your reflections on pages 152-153)

Some final thoughts

We did it! I'm so proud of you for digging in and doing some self-work. I hope you find your journaling time transformative. I'd love to extend you another invitation. Please go to KristyLaschober.com and sign up to receive weekly emails. I'll be sending simple, tangible tools to slay your day, and also give updates about future projects. We are just getting to know each other and I'm hopeful we can grow into an amazing and powerful community. When women on a healing journey get together, it's the most beautiful experience ever. We grow faster, get braver, and do things we've never thought possible.

Before you close this book, consider flipping back through the pages and read the questions again. Did you answer them? Were there any pages you didn't fill out? I challenge you to go back and set aside some time to work on them. Give yourself and your answers lots of grace.

And a little side note - Pay attention to your body as you write and discover parts of yourself. It's not uncommon to feel tired, down or even a little chilled for a short period of time. You may want to seek therapy to help you process all that you will uncover. Writing and reliving all of these very powerful moments will bring you deeper into yourself. Slight flu-like symptoms may arise as you write about triggers or traumatic events from the past. This is a wonderful time to be super kind to yourself. Watch how hard it is to stay present. Are you listening to your body tell you that it's tired? Can you rest without having to explain it to anyone? I still find this challenging. When can you give yourself permission to be still? No one else is going to do it.

Thank you for trusting me. I hope to connect with you soon.

Love,

Kristy

Journaling Section

How did you enter this world?

When did you begin believing certain things about yourself?

How does this affect your life?

What pain or trauma did you experience as a child?

What tools did you use to survive?

Do you still use those tools and do they still serve you?

What new insight do you have thinking back on those days? Is this connecting any dots for you?

Write about it all with lots of GRACE and no judgment.

What do you remember most about your teenage years?
Were you rebellious?
Did you follow the rules? Why?
What was your motivation for the way you lived your life?
Did adults take advantage of you, with or without you realizing it?

How did you navigate life with uncomfortable emotions?
What were the ups and downs of your experience?
What were your examples of marriage?
How did you approach your partnerships?

How do other people see you?
Does it line up with who you actually are?
What parts of you do you hide?

What do you do when you are faced with something painful?

How easily do you have access to your emotions?

What are those emotions?

What emotions have you thrown away a long time ago?

Can you recall a time when you said okay to something you knew you shouldn't have?

What was your motivation?

Were the consequences high?

How long did it take to recover from that decision?

How have you experienced addiction?

Did the magnitude of bad choices ever hit you?

How did you block it out?

Did someone close to you ever make bad choices?
How did you deal with it?

Are you open to new opportunities presented to you?
Write about a time you took a risk and said YES.
What impact did it have?

Write about a time you were facing the unknown or faced circumstances that were out of your control.

How did you feel?

What did you do?

Write about a time someone unexpectedly showed you kindness.

Have you ever had to make an unusual place a home?

Write about a particularly poignant moment, when you knew you should stop a behavior.

Does this quote ring true?

"I know I'm doing something wrong and I feel guilty but neither of those things matter enough for me to stop"

Do you know that you are fearfully and wonderfully made?

What feelings does that evoke?

What parts of you are obviously wonderful?

Have you ever found yourself back in a place you never thought you'd go?

Do you believe in a power bigger than yourself?
Do you have the freedom to form your own belief about God?
Can you access peace whenever you want?

Do you have a friend or family member you trust?

Can you think of a time you experienced love, acceptance, and worthiness?

Are you carrying secrets that weigh you down?

Who is a person that will help you carry your load?

Why are you hiding?

What were some of the poor choices you made that affected others?
Do you think about that in your current interactions with people?

Write about a time that a song, or a certain kind of music touched you deeply. Are you in touch with yourself enough to make choices that will help you?

Write about the last time you were furious.
Did your anger surprise you?
Have you been able to let that go?
Have you ever felt like something was wrong with you?

When was the last time you purposefully shifted your perception?
Do you need to get into acceptance about something right now?

Have you ever had a spiritual experience?
Could the best version of yourself be considered God?
How did you get through an excruciating experience?
Do you know that you are a bad-ass?

Write about a time you were embarking on a new chapter of your life. Was it what you expected?

Has your life ever been in a holding pattern?
What did you do in the waiting?
Do you have a sense of urgency to be courageous?

What makes it hard for you to be completely authentic in front of others?

In what one area can you begin being authentic?

Who is your authentic self?

Which person in your life knows you the best?

Write about a time you persevered through something scary. Did somebody unexpectedly help you through it?

What relationship do you have that brings tension?

Have you tried to start over and engage in a current relationship?

Can you let the past hurts of that relationship go?

Write about a time you were so excited and proud of yourself.

What were the emotions you felt?

Do you still take time to acknowledge your successes?

Have you ever felt the weight of letting go of the past?
What actions did you take to move forward?

Write about a trip you went on with a friend. What was most memorable?

Who are your most beautiful connections with?

Are you taking full responsibility for how your life is going?

What are some of the things stirring in your heart and soul, you have yet to address?

What stops you from saying yes?

What does achievement and success look like to you?

How diverse is your friend circle?
Do you have friends from different cultures?
What interests you about other cultures?

Do you have a mentor?

Are you a mentor to someone else?

What steps could you take to find a mentor?

What are some of the biases you have?

Who do you direct your biggest judgment toward?

What part of your disowned self are you judging?

What have I discovered about myself?

What perceived, shameful experiences can I use to catapult me to greatness?

What do I have to offer that other people around me don't?

Who can I call to ask them to walk on this new vulnerable path with me?

Who is my most free friend?

What makes them so free?

How can I lean into freedom more?

Made in United States
Troutdale, OR
06/10/2023